The Eve of Seven Fishes

The Eve of Seven Fishes

Christmas Cooking In The Peasant Tradition

Robert A. Germano

iUniverse, Inc.
New York Lincoln Shanghai

The Eve of Seven Fishes
Christmas Cooking In The Peasant Tradition

iUniverse books may be ordered through booksellers or by contacting:

iUniverse
2021 Pine Lake Road, Suite 100
Lincoln, NE 68512
www.iuniverse.com
1-800-Authors (1-800-288-4677)

ISBN-13: 978-0-595-36510-4 (pbk)
ISBN-13: 978-0-595-67383-4 (cloth)
ISBN-13: 978-0-595-80943-1 (ebk)
ISBN-10: 0-595-36510-8 (pbk)
ISBN-10: 0-595-67383-X (cloth)
ISBN-10: 0-595-80943-X (ebk)

Printed in the United States of America

BIOGRAPHY

Born in Greensburg, Pa., I grew up in the section of the city known as "Hilltop" or Little Italy.

As a child, I would go to DeBone's Market or DeLallo's Market with my mother to buy the ingredients for the meal known to all Italians as the 'Eve of Seven Fishes.' I remember watching my mother and Grandpap, whose house we lived in, prepare the fish and other items to compliment the feast we were going to devour on Christmas Eve.

After college, I located in Fairmont, WV and started my career in outside sales. I always returned home to enjoy the meal served on the Eve before Christmas and to take the 'bus trip' with my cousins. The bus trip started at 1:00 AM on Christmas morning and lasting until daylight. Re-starting the 'bus trip' again at 3:30 PM on Christmas day to make sure we visited all our relatives by midnight. As a child, I watched my aunts, uncles and older cousins pay this kind of tribute to my Grandpap who never left the dining room table until they all paid their respects. The tradition of the 'bus trip' still goes on but the relatives are fewer and the nighttime run has ceased.

Surfing the net, I located a relative-Memena-on my father's side of the family through one of her friends Angela Sanzo. After several e-mail conversations, I made the decision to discover my roots and took my first journey to Cercemaggiore, Italy in 2001.

Once there I got kidnapped, the red carpet was extended and I had to eat at everyone's house. The simplicity of the meals is remarkable and the flavors are in full bloom. Plus, their wine encouraged me to start making my own wine by purchasing the juice from the provincial grapes of the region.

As I became one of 'the oldest on the block', I wanted to make sure the tradition of Christmas Eve lived on for future generations. Accomplishing this was a little difficult. As I sought out the recipes, I realized it was a little bit of this and a little bit of that or until it looks right! (Madonñ!)

With a lot of laughter and a little bit of arguing (what Italians are known for), I was able to write this cooking reference book for you to enjoy with recipes centered around the simple Italian meal prepared on Christmas Eve.

Despite the distance to the homeland, I yearn to get back to the hills of my ancestors and the exquisite simplicity of the lifestyle they so dearly enjoy. The people of Cercemaggiore are always eager to remind me, Americans are only worried about how high their grass is!

Buona Fortuna e Buona Cottura,

—Robert A. Germano

CONTENTS

Appetizers:

Soups:

First Course:

Second Course: (Fish and Meat)

Second Course: (Vegetables)

Salads:

Desserts:

Miscellaneous:

SECTIONS

INTRODUCTION

(Part One)

This book is not a cookbook with fancy ingredients or recipes with fancy titles. This cookbook is about the Cercesi people, the practical cuisine of my peasant heritage and to honor my ancestors for their holiday traditions, who came to this country from the Campobasso Province in the Molise Region of Italy.

The Eve of Seven Fishes was written and contains cooking instructions generations old going back to the basic and simplistic recipes from the mountains of south central Italy. The Roman Empire, one of the first civilizations who used slaves and peasants to conquer the known world, taught the world how to cook using the simplified methods of peasant food preparation, which brings out the true flavors in Italian cooking.

The Italian kitchen has always been the heart of the Italian home. Today with the 'open' concept in home construction, it has become the den, the area of entertainment (mostly for riddle solving and arguing with Uncle Tony), the gossip room and the living room.

The following pages will take you back to Christmas Eve, at 'Casa delle Nonne'—Granma's House—and that special kind of happiness my Italian family shared before and after midnight mass.

Why Seven Fishes? No one actually knows why the traditional dinner, on the eve before Christmas, consists of Seven Fishes but in keeping with the heritage of the southern Italian home here are some reasons or theories.

First, one would say 'seven' stands for the Seven Sacraments and others would say its meaning goes with the Seven Gifts of the Holy Ghost. For others 'seven' means the Seven Hills of Rome and for another family it's meaning comes from the days it took Mary and Joseph to travel to Bethlehem.

No matter which reason or theory you believe in, the 'Eve of Seven Fishes' was a meatless meal along the lines of meatless Fridays in accordance with the Roman Catholic beliefs for a Virgil of abstinence to show your faith in God and his teachings.

May I also suggest for your complete enjoyment the regional or provincial wines to compliment your first experience in the time-tested art of peasant culinary cooking?

The Eve of Seven Fishes includes a special recipe for assembling the after dinner liquor known as Limoncino, the definition and uses of Grappa, the famous foods from each region in Italy and I included a page of Italian proverbs for your enjoyment.

On each recipe page, the Italian word for each ingredient is listed first with the English equivalent in parentheses.

Christmas Eve in the Italian Tradition cast a very special kind of happiness whether you are young or old. No wonder, nothing is more tantalizing than the smell of garlic and fish cooking or the look of the plated table so beautifully set with the colors of Christmases past.

I hope you enjoy these simple recipes.

Buon Appetito e Buon Natale.

—Robert A. Germano

THE SEVEN FISHES

(I Sette Pesci)

- Anchovy
- Cod
- Tuna
- Whiting
- Haddock
- Smelts
- Squid (Not Really a Fish)

The Seven Fishes

The different regions of Italy all lay claims to serving the best food and it is this regional pride that will select the various fishes served on Christmas Eve.

The Cercesi people and the people from the Campobasso Province used the following for their traditional meal.

First the **Anchovy**, the small, marine and herring like fish found in the Mediterranean Sea. Anchovies are used as an appetizer, the main ingredient for flavoring spaghetti or as a topping on a salad of oranges and hard-boiled eggs. They are often preserved in oil and used in spreads or packaged in paste form. Anchovies are about four inches long, inhabit warm seas, and are chiefly valuable as food for other fishes. You will find recipes that eliminate the saltiness and bring out the fragrant Anchovy taste enjoyed by Italians for each course to be prepared on Christmas Eve.

For frying or preparing a casserole, the Codfish is used. **Cods** are bottom-feeders with soft fins. The large ventral fins are located under or in front of the pectorals rather than behind them as in other fishes and their average weight are ten to twenty-five pounds. Off shore cod rarely exceeds forty inches in length. In shore cod are smaller reaching twelve pounds and thirty-four inches. If you have a family of big eaters, like my cousin Vinnie (doesn't every Italian family have a cousin Vinnie), you'll need to buy about ten pounds of Cod (Baccala), but if they eat like a bird, like my mom, you're only going to need four pounds. Then there's Vinnie's sister who doesn't like fish, so if you are not a fish eater then you can just 'fuhgedaboudit'.

Next, you'll need to buy **Tuna** for making the meatless spaghetti sauce. Tunas inhabit temperate and tropical seas. They have streamlined bodies with two fins and five or more finlets on the back. The body is very narrow in the tail region and the tail is deeply forked. Tuna is the largest member of the Mackerel family. Certain species can grow up to sixty pounds but don't tell my cousin Vinnie. Use about two cans of Tuna per pound of pasta or 'macaroni' for you Italians.

Now it's time to talk soup or don't get to close to Granma when she has a wooden spoon in her hand. This is usually the time when all nosy boys got their first knot on the head. As you got older, lets say about seven, you were as tall as your Granma (even though she wore those ugly square heeled black shoes) and she quit hitting you. Speaking of Granma's, why did they wear their nylons rolled down around their ankles? Lets move on.

Whiting is my family's choice for assembling soup. Whiting are a slender, carnivorous, spiny-finned food fish and a member of the Cod family. Whiting average three pounds in weight and grow to about two feet in length. If Whiting isn't available, it can be replaced with Orange Ruffy. I never heard of that fish until I was in my twenties. How about you other Italians?

Another fish for battering and frying is the **Haddock**, also a member of the Cod family and the most important food fish of Atlantic and European waters. Haddocks are also bottom-feeders. They are smaller than cods, reaching five pounds and a length of two feet and have black lateral lines and dark side patches.

Next is the fish of all fishes and the reason I composed this cookbook. **The Smelt**. This past Christmas my best friend Bill wasn't able to have Smelts on Christmas Eve. I decided to bring him these tasty little treats (that are eaten like popcorn) while we watched the bowl games on New Years Day. Smelts are a variety of small, silvery food fishes closely allied to the grayling of the salmon family. Known for their fragrant flesh, they grow to about three or four inches in length. Smelts are battered, fried to a golden brown and can become habit forming. I think we polished off two pounds within five minutes.

Now it's time for the fish that's not a fish. **The Squid.** If it comes out of the water, it's a fish to the Italian peasants. So don't worry about it or I'll send my cousin Vinnie to your house. Squid is a carnivorous marine cephalopod mollusk used for sautéing in olive oil as an appetizer, for flavoring the spaghetti sauce, to stuff as one of the main dishes or used as the main ingredient for Insulata di Mare. Squid is a favorite food along the Amalfi Coast in the Campania region. Species of Squid range in size from two inches to a total length of fifty-nine feet.

MY HERITAGE

(La Mia Editá)

Regional Map

Ancestry

Around 1900 A.D. my ancestors came seeking escape from a peasant existence for a livelihood insuring new found self-respect and human dignity. From Cercemaggiore (Molise) Italy, a tiny village clinging to the side of the south central Apennine Mountains, my Grandfathers' and Grandmothers' settled in S.W. Pennsylvania, their newly adopted land, and started new families. Never giving up their cherished ties to the Mother Land and with inner strength and pride, they instilled in their off springs their traditions and customs. The 'Cercesi' people also brought with them the recipes for celebrating on the eve before Christmas and just as my parents learned from them, this cookbook is for succeeding generations to learn the art of preparing simple dishes in the Cercemaggiore tradition.

Molise

After the fall of the Roman Empire in 476 A.D., Molise was invaded by the Goths (535 A.D.) and then by the Languebards (or Lombards) in 572, and annexed to the Dukedom of Benevento. A very troubled period began with the invasions of the Saracens, which in 860 A.D. destroyed Isernia, Telese, Alife, Sepino, Boiano and Venafro. By the 10th century there were 9 countdoms: Venafro, Larino, Trivento, Bojano, Isernia, Campomarino, Termoli, Sangro, Pietrabbondante. In 1095 the most powerful of them, Bojano, came under the rule of the Norman Hugo I of Molhouse, who most probably gave his name to the region. His successor Ugo II was Count of Molise in 1144. In the 16th century Molise was included to the Province of Capitanata (Apulia) and in 1806 became an autonomous Province, included in the Abruzzi region. In the 19th century there was a great worsening of the economic conditions of the population, and this gave rise under the newly established Kingdom of Italy (1861) to brigandage and a massive emigration not only abroad but also to more industrial Italian areas. A heavy destruction took place in WW2, until finally the Allied Forces were able to land at Termoli, in September 1943.

Molise is the youngest Italian region, since it was established in 1963, when the region "Abruzzo e Molise" was split into two regions, today they still maintain a common identity both geographically and in their historical and traditional heritage. The region is administratively divided into two Provinces, Campobasso, the regional capital, and Isernia, and comprises 136 municipalities, most of them very small, but each unique and worth seeing. Molise is mostly mountainous and the economy, in the past centuries, was highly dependent on the transit of shepherds and their flocks from Abruzzo to Apulia. Molise still relies heavily on agriculture and livestock rising, though the food and garment industries are undergoing a remarkable development.

Within Molise lies the four small hamlets or villages of my ancestry. They are Cercemaggiore, Riccia, Sepino and Gildone. Of these villages, three of my grandparents came from Cercemaggiore and one of my grandmothers came from Gildone but the recipes that follow have traditional ties to all four villages.

Cercemaggiore

Province of Campobasso, Molise—Italy

Only twenty-five kilometers from Campobasso, this ancient town rises on an elevated position, overlooking the Tammaro Valley, the Matese and the Majella, and southwards as far as the Mountains of the Salerno area. The name derives either from Quercus Maior (meaning big oak) or from the Arabic "cerce", meaning rock. It was inhabited since pre-historic times, and then was a center of the Samnites, a fierce, warlike Italic people, who fought courageously against the Romans before being conquered. It was also occupied by the Saracens, and later, in the 11th century, by the Normans. It is today a favorite starting point for those who love trekking and horse riding along the ancient "tratturi" of the Sannio.

Riccia

Province of Campobasso, Molise—Italy

Archeological findings in the territory show the presence of a Samnite settlement followed then by the establishment of a Roman colony. After the dark period of the Middle Ages, Riccia was always a fiefdom of the de Capua family. A famous figure in the history of Riccia was Costanza di Chiaromonte, wife of King Ladislaw of Durazzo, who was rejected by her husband in 1392. She was taken as a wife by Andrea de Capua, from which union two sons were born. The unfortunate queen's sepulchre is in the Church of Santa Maria delle Grazie.

Sepino

Province of Campobasso, Molise—Italy

In the middle of the uncontaminated, green valley of the Tammaro River surrounded by the Matese mountains, Sepino is also a repository of thousands of years of glory, which make it a perfect destination for the lovers of nature and history. In the area called Terravecchia, there was a prehistoric settlement of the early shepherds of the Bronze Age. Then there rose the powerful ancient Samnite town of Ocre Saepinatz, one of the last in Italy to surrender to the Romans in 293 B.C. In the vicinity one of the best-preserved dinosaurs in Europe was found.

Gildone

Province of Campobasso, Molise—Italy

Inhabited since very ancient times, as shown by a Samnite necropolis in the area called Morgia. Gildone had a great importance in the Middle Ages thanks to its powerful lords, Rao Falco Graone, Cardinal Orsini, the Sanfromondo family and Pope Benedict XII, who came here to consecrate the churches of San Sabino and Sant'Antonio Abate.

Regional Foods

(Alimenti Regionale)

Valle D'Aosta/Piedmont—Polenta, Bagna Cauda, Tartufi Bianchi, Zambaione.

Liquria—Ravioli, Pasta con Pesto, Cima, Pandolce.

Tuscany—Crostini, Ribollita, Cacciuco, Bistecca Fiorentini.

Umbria—Finocchiona, Tartufi Neri, Biroldo Colce, Cioccolata di Perugia.

Latium—Pinzimonio, Pasta alla Carbonara, Carriofi alla Guidea, Saltimbocca.

Campania—Mozzarella, Cannelloni, Calamari, Pizza Margherita.

Sardinia—Cassola, Bottarga, Porceddu, Pecorino.

Sicily—Caponata, Pasta con le Sarde, Farsumagru, Cannoli.

Calabria—Melazane al Funghetto, Zuppa di Pesce, Salciccia Calabrese, Provolone.

Basilicata—Capocollo, Luganega, Peperonata, Panzarotti.

Apulia—Olio d'Oliva, Calsone, Laganelle al Arguilia, Caciocavalle.

Abruzzo/Molise—Bruschetta, Diavolichio, Maccheroni alla Chitarra, Scamorza.

Marches—Musciolialla Marinara, Brodetto, Porchetta, Stoccafisso in Umido.

Emilia-Romagna—Prosciutto, Tortellini, Bollito Misto, Formaggio Parmigiano.

Veneto/Friuli-Venezia Giulia—Carpaccio, Risie Bisi, Fegato alla Veneziana, Tiramisu.

Lombardy/Trentino Alto Adige—Risotto, Minestrone, Ossobuco, Gorgonzola.

THE BASICS

(I Principi Fondamentali)

Getting Started
(Ottenere Iniziato)

Lets assume you want to become an Italian cook. What should you have in your kitchen (cucina)? First, you need two large pots, two wooden spoons, a colander, an iron skillet (seasoned), a good nose and a great pair of hands.

Fresh ingredients will give you the finest quality end product that you can proudly serve in the traditional, exquisite simplicity that is the hallmark of peasant foods throughout south central Italy. Therefore, use fresh vegetables, fruits, and herbs when possible. Secondly, a bottle of extra virgin olive oil, red and white wine (Montepulciano and Moscato), and three types of vinegar—red and white wine vinegar and balsamic are historic staples. To season always use fresh ground black pepper and either kosher or sea salt.

The heart of the Italian cupboard (armadietto) has many different types of pasta including dattalini or anici di pepe (for soups), cavatelli or penne (for thicker red sauces), cappellini (for light red sauces or with oil sauces) and fettucine (for cream sauces) and one must not forget to have plenty of **Peccorino Romano** and **Parmesan Reggiano** cheeses to complete that infinite variety of flavorful dishes you are about to experience.

Moving on to the refrigerator (frigorifero), the number one staple is the garlic. Garlic is used in just about all meals except desserts and you can grow your own. Garlic is generally planted in October and is harvested in July.

The appetizer (antipasto) as with most meals at the peasant table is one of cured meats and cheeses. To start you must have salami, cappacola, soprassata, and prosciutto to be served along side of fontinella, asiago, provolone, and gorgonzola on separate plates for each guest—but never on Christmas

Eve! Today at some delis, a combination of Italian meats and cheeses can be bought rolled together for slicing and serving.

To complement and put the final touch to any Italian meal or to garnish, you will need the following herbs, roasted red peppers, oil cured black or green Italian olives and in the cellar (cantina) you must have jars of marinated peppers and/or marinated vegetables.

Herbs

(Erbe)

Basil (Basilico) is a member of the mint family that is highly aromatic, sweet and peppery. Basil is one of the main ingredients in a pesto sauce. It is said that if an Italian woman placed a sprig of basil on her balcony, it was a message to her male friend that he could call that evening.

Italian Parsley (Prezzimolo) is a southern European herb that is slightly peppery and more favorable than its curled cousin. Parsley is also great as a mouth freshener as it masks the odor of garlic.

Oregano (Origano) is also related to the mint family plus the thyme family. This herb actually gets stronger in flavor when dried and is used more commonly in southern Italian cooking.

Rosemary (Rosmarino) is used as a seasoning for roasts, potatoes, bread and vegetables. Fresh rosemary has a strong aroma when picked but mellows when used in cooking. In the olden days it was used for medicinal purposes.

Sage (Salvia) often used with rosemary to flavor meat dishes, sage is generally used in northern Italy. As part of an antipasto, you can dip sage leaves in a light batter and fry in oil olive and serve with Montepulciano.

Appetizers
(Antipasto)

Ingredients:

Marinated Vegetables

Prosciutto

Cappacola

Soprassata

Salami

Fontinella

Asiago

Provolone

Gorgonzola

Pepe Rossi Arrostiti (Roasted Red Peppers)

Olive Curate Olio (Oil cured olives)

Slice prosciutto, cappicolla, soprassata, salami wafer thin, cut roasted red peppers into large julienne strips, cut fontinella, asiago, provolone, goronzola cheese into thick slices or cubes. Arrange on small plate and garnish with marinated vegetables and oil cured olives.

This appetizer is served before meals or as a snack in the evening when friends or family stop in for a visit. Remember to serve it with a dry red wine like Montepulciano and fresh Italian bread.

Marinated Peppers

(Peperone Marinate)

Ingredients:

Peperoni (Red & Green Peppers)	6–8 Medium
Aglio (Garlic)	2 ½ cloves
Olivo di Oliva (Olive Oil)	5 tsp
Aceto (Vinegar)	1 qt
Zuchhero (Sugar)	2 cups
Aqua (Water)	1 cup
Sale (Salt)	½ tsp
Caldi del pepe (Hot Pepper Flakes)	To Taste

Cut the peppers into large cubes and place in a large bowl. Bring to boil all other ingredients. Boil for 5 minutes. Pour hot mixture over the peppers and marinate for 36 hours in refrigerator. Unused peppers can be stored in mason jars in refrigerator.

Optional: When making months in advance, divide peppers, garlic, olive oil, salt and hot pepper flakes into five mason jars (pints). Boil for five minutes the vinegar, sugar and water and pour into heated jars, seal and turn upside down.

Marinated Vegetables

(Verdure Marinate)

Ingredients:

Cavolfiore (Cauliflower)	1 Cup
Peperoni (Red & Green Peppers)	1 Cup
Olive Nere (Black Olives)	1 Cup
Funghi si Abbottona (Mushroom Buttons)	1 Cup
Olive Verdi (Green Olives)	1 Cup
Cuori del Carciofo (Artichoke Hearts)	1 Cup
Aglio (Garlic)	4 Cloves
Olio di Oliva (Olive Oil)	2 Tsp.
Sale (Salt)	To Taste
Pepe Nero (Black pepper)	To Taste
Aceto (Vinegar)	1 ½ Qts.
Zucchero Sugar)	1 Cup

Together bring to boil in a pot vinegar, oil, garlic, sugar, salt and pepper. Combine vegetables in bowl, pour hot mixture over and marinate for 30 to 36 hours in the refrigerator. Drain and serve on a large platter—family style.

Salted Cod

(Baccala)

Growing up, I would always go with my mother to the market and before the Christmas Holiday we would shop for the ingredients to assemble the meal served on Christmas Eve.

There were two ingredients she purchased at either DeBone's (DiBona's) or DeLallo's Market that were dry and hard as rocks. One came in a wooden crate and the other in a wooden barrel.

Both items needed to be soaked in fresh water for seven days and the water <u>must</u> be changed at least two or three times a day.

For those of Italian descent you know the other product to be Lupini Beans—that are eaten by breaking the outer skin with your front teeth and popping the inner bean in your mouth.

Anchovy Sauce

(Salsa del Alici)

This recipe is used to cover the Polpette di Baccala (Baccala Balls) that can be used as an appetizer or cooked directly in the sauce as you would meatballs. This is just another example of the simplicity of cooking in the peasant tradition.

Ingredients:

Alici (Anchovy)	1 Can
Aglio (Garlic)	4 Cloves
Cipolla (Onion)	1 Small
Olio di Oliva (Olive Oil)	3 Oz.
Puré del Pomodoro (Tomato Puree)	15 Oz.
Aqua (Water)	15 Oz.
Pepe Nero (Black Pepper)	To Taste

Sauté minced or sliced garlic and onion in olive oil until translucent (do not burn), add anchovy and coarse black pepper. Stir until anchovies are broken up into small pieces. Stir in tomato puree until heated then add water and blend. Bring to boil stirring occasionally then simmer for about 2–3 hours or until desired thickness.

Optional: Add ¼-cup Moscato wine to onion and garlic before adding the tomato puree and water.

Basic Batter

(Pastella di Base)

The recipe for this batter differs from home to home. Since all of the families did not write down the amounts for each ingredient, the final mixture was always "when it looks right."

You too may have your favorite batter recipe to use when frying but I always enjoyed the 'golden' appearance this batter has to offer.

Before you make any changes, I sincerely hope you give this recipe a try.

Farina (Flour)	1 Cup
Uova (Eggs) beaten	5 Medium
Latte (Milk)	¼ Cup
Sale (Salt)	To Taste
Pepe Nero (Black Pepper)	To Taste
Lievito (Baking Powder)	½ Tsp.

Optional: For a crunchier texture a recipe for using bread crumbs, Romano cheese, and lemon zest is on page 54.

Lemon Liquor

(Limoncino)

This is a recipe for the famous after dinner drink through out all of Italy. This liquor is widely associated with the town of Sorrento in the Campania Region. Sorrento is south of Naples and is one of the great shopping towns for travelers.

Ingredients:

Etanolo (Grain Alcohol)	32 Oz.
Aqua (Water)	22 Oz.
Zucchero (Sugar)	2 lbs.
Limone (Lemon)	8 Medium

Zest the lemons (do not use any of the white next to the lemon meat) and add the zest to the grain alcohol. Cover and let stand for 6–7 days. Next dissolve the sugar in warm water (low heat) till completely absorbed. Let mixture cool to room temperature, combine with alcohol and mix well. Wait 15 minutes and strain. Pour finished product into sanitized bottle and cork.

Menú Di Vigilia Di Natale

Contents

Cercese Digestive

APPETIZER

(ANTIPASTO)

Anchovy and Olive Canapé

(Canapé di Alici e Oliva)

Ingredients:

Alici (Anchovy)	½ Can
Giogo del Uova (Egg Yoke)	One
Oliva Curate Olio (Oil Cured Olives) Pitted	2 ½ Dz.
Burro (Butter) Unsalted	¼ Cup
Parmigiano-Reggiano (Parmesan Cheese)	½ Cup

In a blender put the olives, anchovies, egg, butter and cheese. Puree. If a little dry, moisten with a little more olive oil but not to wet. Spread the mixture on toast points or stale Italian bread and garnish with thin julienne slices of marinated red and green peppers.

Baccala Balls

(Polpette di Baccala)

Ingredients:

Baccala (salted cod) chopped fine	1 lb.
Formaggio del Romano (Romano Cheese)	⅓ C.
Briciole Del Pane (Bread Crumbs)	⅔ C.
Uova (Eggs)	1 Large
Aglio (Garlic)	1 Clove
Salsa del Alici (Anchovy Sauce)	

Mix chopped Baccala, minced garlic, beaten eggs, breadcrumbs and cheese in a large bowl and form into balls. Deep fry in oil at 360 degrees F. Cover with heated anchovy sauce. SEE PAGE 35 or heat in anchovy sauce for 15-20 minutes and serve over cappellini as a first course.

Bread and Salted Water

(Pane e Acquasale)

Ingredients:

Pane (Bread)	1 Loaf (stale)
Aglio (Garlic)	4 Cloves
Olio di Oliva (Olive Oil)	½ Cup
Origano (Oregano)	To Taste
Sale (Salt)	To Taste
Aqua (Water)	

Cut stale Italian Style bread into regular slices. Sprinkle them with ample water to moisten. Arrange on a platter. Crush the garlic and spread it on the bread slices (about ¾ teaspoon per slice.) Dust the slices with oregano and salt to taste. Drizzle the olive oil over the bread evenly. This is an excellent compliment with the meat and cheese antipasto.

Flat Bread Recipe: Mix 1 ¼ tsp. yeast in ½ cup warm water, stir and let rest for 20-30 minutes. Combine 1 ½ cups of 'unbleached' flour and 1 tsp. salt in a bowl. Add yeast mixture and knead until smooth. Set in warm place and let rise for two hours. Spread dough into a greased 9" x 12" pan and bake at 375 degrees F. until golden brown.

Fish Soup

(Minestra dei Pesci)

Ingredients:

Pesce (Whiting Filets or Haddock)	2 lb.
Cavolfiore (Cauliflower)	1 Head
Pomodori Tagliati (Diced Tomatoes)	28 Oz.
Aglio (Garlic)	3 Cloves
Cipolla (Onion)	1 Small
Uva Passa (Raisins)	2 Small Boxes
Sale (Salt)	To Taste
Pepe Nero (Black pepper)	To Taste
Olio di Oliva (Olive Oil)	3 Tbs.
Aqua (Water)	16 Oz.

Pour olive oil in skillet, sauté onions and garlic until translucent (do not burn), add the diced tomatoes and water. Add kosher salt and coarse black to taste. Cook until sauce is done to your liking. Clean, separate and blanch cauliflower in water until tender. Add cauliflower and raisins to the diced tomatoes and bring to boil, cook cauliflower until firm not soft, and then add the fish and finish cooking until fish starts to flake. Serve in a large bowl.

FIRST COURSE
(PRIMO PIATTO)

Spaghetti with Anchovy, Garlic and Oil
(Spaghetti deí Aglio e Olio con Alici)

Ingredients:

Cappellini (Angel Hair Pasta)	1 lb.
Alici (Anchovy)	1 Can
Aglio (Garlic)	4 Cloves
Olio di Oliva (Olive Oil)	3 oz.
Pepe Nero (Black pepper)	To Taste
Prezzimolo (Parsley)	To Garnish
Parmigiano (Parmesan) Grated	To Garnish

Sauté minced or sliced garlic in oil until translucent (do not burn) add anchovies and coarse black pepper, next stir and smash anchovies until they are broken up into small pieces. Pour over cooked al dente pasta, blend and serve immediately. Garnish with Parmesan Reggiano and fresh parsley.

Optional: Add one 15 oz can of tomato puree and one 15 oz can of water to above and simmer for one hour then pour over cooked pasta

Remember; cook all pasta according to the label for al dente texture. Pasta should not be to hard or to soft.

Spaghetti with Tuna Fish or Squid Sauce

(Spaghetti con Salsa del Tonno o del Calamaro)

Ingredients:

Cappellini (Angel Hair Pasta)	1 lb
Tonno o Calamare (Tuna or Squid)	10-12 Oz.
Salsa del Pomodori (Tomato Sauce)	15 oz.
Colla del Pomodori (Tomato Paste)	6 Oz.
Aglio (Garlic)	3 Cloves
Cipolla (Onion)	1 Small
Basilico (Basil)	10 Leaves
Olio di Oliva (Olive Oil)	3 Tbs.
Sugar (Zucchero)	1 Tsp.
Pepe Nero (Black pepper)	To Taste
Sale (Salt)	To Taste
Aqua (Water) For Tomato Sauce	15 Oz.
Aqua (Water) For Tomato Paste	6 Oz.

Sauté finely chopped onion and minced garlic until translucent. Add tomato paste and water. Cook until thoroughly mixed and heated through. Combine tomato sauce, finely chopped basil, water, coarse black pepper, kosher salt and sugar in stockpot. Bring to a boil stirring occasionally then simmer for about two to three hours. Add tuna fish or squid ½ hour before serving to heat through. Pour over cooked pasta, blend and serve.

Optional: Add ½-cup Moscato wine to onion and garlic before adding the paste and water.

Dry Spaghetti

(Spaghetti Asciutti)

Ingredients:

Cappellini (Angel Hair Pasta)	1 lb.
Briciole del Pane (Bread Crumbs)	3 Cups
Uva Passa (Raisins)	Small Box
Noci (Walnuts)	½ Cup
Aglio (Garlic)	2 Cloves
Prezzemolo (Parsley)	2 Tbs.
Scorza Arancione Grattata (Grated Orange Rind)	2 Tbs.
Olio di Oliva (Olive Oil)	¼ Cup
Pepe Nero (Black Pepper)	To Taste

Sauté garlic until translucent, add breadcrumbs and stir until the breadcrumbs are lightly toasted. Add raisins, chopped walnuts, fresh parsley and grated orange rind. If a little dry moisten with more oil. Continue toasting until all ingredients are heated. Prepare pasta according to label directions for al dente texture. Pasta should not be to hard or to soft. Toss pasta and toasted mixture together and serve warm.

SECOND COURSE

(SECONDO PIATTO)

Baccala and Bread Crumbs

(Baccala e Briciole del Pane)

Ingredients:

Baccala (Salted Cod Fish)	2 lbs
Briciole del Pane (Bread Crumbs)	1 Cup
Uva Passa (Raisins)	Small Box
Noci (Walnuts)	1 Cup
Olio di Oliva (Olive Oil)	1 Cup
Sale (Salt)	To Taste
Pepe Nero (Black pepper)	To Taste

Mix breadcrumbs, raisins, and chopped walnuts together. Sprinkled with kosher salt and coarse black pepper to taste. In a casserole dish drizzle a little olive oil, layer the Baccala and breadcrumb mixture. Bake at 350 degrees F. for 25–30 minutes. Stir occasionally.

Stuffed Squid

(Calamaro Farcito)

Ingredients:

Calamaro (Squid)	2 lb.
Briciole del Pane (Bread Crumbs)	¾ Cup
Formaggio del Romano (Romano Cheese)	½ Cup
Uova (Eggs) Beaten	1 Egg
Aglio (Garlic) Minced	2 Cloves
Prezzemolo (Parsley)	2 Tbs.
Basilico (Basil) Chopped	10 Leaves
Pepe Nero (Black pepper)	To Taste
Sale (Salt)	To Taste
Olio di Oliva (Olive Oil)	2 Tbs.

Clean and wash squid. Cut off tentacles. Sauté the tentacles in olive oil for 5 minutes. Combine tentacles (finely chopped) and all other ingredients into bowl until firm. Stuff squid with mixture (do not over stuff as they will explode when baking) and close the opening with a skewer or toothpick. Arrange stuffed squid in a casserole dish and drizzle with a little olive oil. Bake at 350 degrees F. for 35–40 minutes. Cover with heated anchovy sauce (page 35) and serve.

Optional: Arrange stuffed squid in a casserole dish, cover with anchovy sauce and bake at 350 degrees F. for 35–40 minutes.

Note: If mixture a little loose add one more egg. This recipe will stuff up to 10–12 medium to large squid.

Baccala Casserole

(Casseruola di Baccala)

Ingredients:

Baccala (Salted Cod)	2 ½ lbs.
Cavolfiore (Cauliflower)	1 Head
Salsa del Pomodori (Tomato Sauce)	16 oz.
Aglio (Garlic)	3 Cloves
Cipolla (Onion)	1 Small
Olio di Oliva (Olive Oil)	2 Tbs.
Pepe Nero (Black pepper)	To Taste
Sale (Salt)	To Taste
Aqua (Water)	8 oz.

Sauté minced or sliced garlic and onion in oil until translucent (do not burn). Add tomato sauce, water and cauliflower and cook until cauliflower is firm. Put the Baccala in a casserole dish and pour in the sauce and bake in the oven for 20–25 minutes at 350 degrees F.

Optional: Add one small box of raisins to the Baccala before adding the sauce.

Broccoli Casserole

(Casseruola di Broccolo)

Ingredients:

Broccolo (Broccoli)	1 Bunch
Briciole Del Pane (Bread Crumbs)	1 Cup
Formaggio del Romano (Romano Cheese)	½ Cup
Uva Passa (Raisins)	Small Box
Noci (Walnuts)	1 Cup
Aglio (Garlic)	2 Cloves
Olio di Oliva (Olive Oil)	3 Tbs.
Pepe Nero (Black pepper)	To Taste
Sale (Salt)	To Taste

Separate and wash the broccoli, then blanche in water until tender. Mix breadcrumbs, cheese, raisins, walnuts (coarse chopped), chopped garlic, kosher salt and coarse black pepper. Layer in a baking dish and drizzle with oil and cover. Bake at 350 degrees F. for 20–25 minutes.

Fried Smelts

(Sperlani Fritti)

Ingredients:

Sperlani (Smelts)	2 lbs.
Farina (Flour)	1 Cup
Uova (Eggs)	5 Medium
Latte (Milk)	¼ Cup
Sale (Salt)	To Taste
Pepe Nero (Black pepper)	To Taste
Lievito (Baking Powder)	½ Tsp.

Combine 1-cup flour, 5 medium eggs (beaten), and ¼ cup milk in large bowl. Add ½ teaspoon baking powder, kosher salt, coarse black pepper and mix well.

Wash and clean smelts. Dredge in basic batter and fry in oil in large iron skillet until golden brown.

Optional: You may butterfly smelts and remove the backbone before frying. Also, you may refrigerate coated smelts the night before frying.

Fried Baccala and Haddock

(Baccala e Haddock Fritti)

Ingredients:

Baccala (Salted Cod) and Haddock	1 lb each
Farina (Flour)	1 Cup
Uova (Eggs)	5 Medium
Latte (Milk)	¼ Cup
Sale (Salt)	To Taste
Pepe Nero (Black pepper)	To Taste
Lievito (Baking Powder)	½ Tsp.

Cut Baccala and haddock into 2 ½ inch pieces. Combine 1-cup flour, 5 medium eggs (beaten), and ¼ cup milk in large bowl. Add ½ teaspoon baking powder, kosher salt, coarse black pepper and mix well. Dredge in basic batter and fry in oil in large iron skillet until golden brown.

Briciole del Pane (Bread Crumbs)	1 Cup
Formaggio del Romano (Romano Cheese)	½ Cup
Limone (Lemon) Grated	1 Small

Method Two: Dredge in basic batter and coat with breadcrumbs that have been seasoned with Romano cheese and grated lemon zest.

Fried Cauliflower

(Cavolfiore Fritti)

Ingredients:

Cavolfiore (Cauliflower)	1 Head
Farina (Flour)	1 Cup
Uova (Eggs)	5 Medium
Latte (Milk)	¼ Cup
Sale (Salt)	To Taste
Pepe Nero (Black pepper)	To Taste
Lievito (Baking Powder)	½ Tsp.

First clean and separate the cauliflower into florets. Blanche in water until tender and firm, not soft. Drain. Combine 1-cup flour, 5 medium eggs (beaten), and ¼ cup milk in large bowl. Add ½ teaspoon baking powder, kosher salt, coarse black pepper and mix well. Dredge in basic batter and fry in oil in large iron skillet until golden brown. Remember, you can do this the night before and refrigerate between layers of plastic wrap.

SALADS

(INSALATE)

Tossed Salad Family Style

(Insalata Stile Mista della Famiglia)

Ingredients:

Romaine lattuga (Lettuce)	1 Head
Pomodori (Tomatoes)	3 Small
Cipolla (Onion)	1 Small
Peperone Rossi (Red Pepper)	1 Medium
Sedano (Celery)	2 Ribs
Aglio (Garlic)	1 Clove
Sale (Salt)	To Taste
Pepe Nero (Black pepper)	To Taste
Olio e Aceto (Oil and Vinegar)	

Put lettuce, quartered tomatoes (cut in half), thinly sliced onions, cubed peppers, chopped celery and minced garlic in large bowl add the kosher salt and course black pepper. Combine 5 oz. olive oil, 2 oz. white wine vinegar and a ¼ oz. of the balsamic vinegar shake vigorously and pour enough to coat all of the ingredients. Toss with your hands, taste to see if it needs re-seasoned with salt or pepper then place on the dinner table, family style.

Baccala (Salted Cod) Salad

(Insalata di Baccala)

Ingredients:

Baccala (cooked and shredded)	1 ½ lb.
Peperoni (Red & Green Peppers) (Cured in vinegar)	1 Cup
Sedano (Celery)	1 Cup
Fogli del Sedano (Celery leaves)	1 Cup
Olive Nere (Black Olives)	1 Cup
Aglio (Garlic)	3 Cloves
Pepe Nero (Black pepper)	To Taste
Basilico (Basil)	10 Leaves
Olio di Oliva (Olive Oil)	¾ Cup

Cook Baccala for four minutes in boiling water, cool and shred. Combine with red and green peppers, celery, celery leaves, black olives and garlic that have been finely chopped. Sprinkle with coarse black pepper, chopped fresh basil and drizzle with olive oil. Refrigerate on a platter covered until cold or when ready to serve.

Oranges and Egg Salad

(Insalata di Aranci e Uovo)

Ingredients:

Fette Arancioni (Orange Slices)	2 Naval
Fette Uova (Hard Boiled Egg Slices)	3 Large
Alici (Anchovy)	1 Jar
Olive Nero (Small Black Olives)	1 Can
Pepe Nero (Black Pepper)	To Taste
Olio di Oliva (Olive Oil)	3 Tbs.

Arrange orange slices (¼ inch thick) on a platter. Place a slice of hard boiled egg in the center of each orange slice. Place a ½ anchovy on the egg slice. Dot the platter with black olives (after they have been rinsed and drained) then drizzle with olive oil. Sprinkle with coarse black pepper.

GET READY FOR THIS HOLIDAY TREAT? THIS DISH IS SERVED AT THE END OF THE MEAL AND THE HARD BOILED EGG WITH ANCHOVY COMPLEMENT EACH OTHER VERY WELL. SAVE THE ORANGE SLICE UNTIL LAST IT MAKES AN EXCELLENT PALATE CLEANSER.

MY FAMILY SERVES THIS SALAD AT EVERY HOLIDAY MEAL, IT IS BELIEVED TO HAVE BEEN FIRST SERVED DURING A WAKE.

DESSERT

(DOLCI)

Christmas Star

(Stella di Natale)

Ingredients:

Uova (Eggs)	5 Large
Burro (Butter)	1 ⅓ Stick
Zucchero (Sugar)	1 Cup
Nocciole (Almonds or Hazelnuts)	1 Cup
Cioccolato (Bittersweet Chocolate)	½ Cup
Farina (Flour)	½ Cup
Lievito (Baking Powder)	½ Tbs.

Separate the egg yokes from the whites. Mix in bowl over hot water (double boiler) with the sugar. Add to that the butter, which has been melted, the flour, the baking powder, the finely chopped nuts and the bittersweet chocolate. Mix well. Beat the egg whites until firm and fluffy. Fold the egg whites in to the batter gently. Pour into a star shaped pan or star shaped cookie molds that have been greased and dusted with flour. Bake at 350 degrees F. for 40 minutes. Once star has been cooled, sprinkle with sugar and serve.

The Waffles

(I Ferratelle)

Ingredients:

Oova (Eggs)	6 Large
Zucchero (Sugar)	1 Cup
Vaniglia (Vanilla)	1–2 Teaspoons
Burro (Butter) Melted	1 Cup
Farina (Flour)	3 ½ Cups
Lievito (Baking Powder)	4 Tsp.

Make a well in the flour. Add the eggs that have been beaten, the butter that has been melted and cooled, the vanilla and the sugar. Knead all ingredients together to form smooth dough. Cut into small to medium pieces (or teaspoon size) and cook in a pizzelle iron.

Optional: Increase sugar to 2 cups or for a more traditional recipe replace vanilla with anise oil.

INTRODUCTION

(Part Two)

Get ready for some more serious eating. Traditionally, the main meal on Christmas Day is served at either noon or 1:00 pm. and the same holds true for all holidays and Sundays.

This meal consists of simple courses and all the leftovers from the night before. Listed first will be the traditional recipes to make your own pasta, meatballs and spaghetti sauce. These recipes you must master. They are the staple foods for every Sunday meal.

The traditional antipasto of Peasant Style Greased Bread along with cured lunchmeats (growing up I thought all lunchmeats ended in a vowel) and cheeses are served. Speaking of lunchmeats, I spent my entire childhood calling lunchmeats and bread 'sangwiches'.

Only during this festive holiday, Italians everywhere will experience the phenomena of twenty to thirty people (all with last names ending in a vowel), fitting into a twenty-five square foot dining room (small children had to eat in the kitchen) talking as loud as they can because it is normal. Something outsiders do not understand. Being of Italian descent, this is what it is all about and why being back home for the simple traditional meals served during this holiday is almost more important than going to church.

When Christmas fell on Sunday, our afternoons and evenings, like all Sundays, were spent visiting my grandparents on my mother's side and my extended family. Extended families are the relatives who aren't really your relatives and as a child you didn't realize this until you were old enough to drink wine. Of course, your first glass of wine was before you were a teenager thanks to Grandpap. Also, Sunday night at Granma's house the floor was filled with kids and the chairs filled with adults watching the Lawrence Welk and the Ed Sullivan shows.

Now, you should understand why the holidays are so special, why relatives will travel great distances, and why every meal had to be eaten with a hunk of bread in your left hand.

After today, Italians everywhere long for next years feast and all the preparations that has to be done to enjoy this once a year traditional culinary extravaganza.

—Robert A. Germano

More Basics

(Piú Principi Fondamentali)

Pasta Recipe

(Ricetta della Pasta)

This recipe is also a tried and true mixture of basic ingredients that never fails. And you never have to worry about making too much, just get your basic shirt box and layer pasta between wax paper and place in freezer.

Ingredients:

Farina (Flour)	3 ½ Cups
Uova (Eggs)	3 Eggs (Beaten)
Aqua (Water)	As Needed

In a bowl make a well in the flour, add beaten eggs and form dough by hand. Adding ice water, if necessary, to moisten. Knead well until elastic and smooth. Cover and let rest at room temperature for 15 minutes. Roll out dough to about ¼ inch thickness or to size of pasta you desire. Cut dough to Cappellini size, dust with flour and separate.

Spaghetti Sauce

(Salsa degli Spaghetti)

The secret to all spaghetti sauce is to braise pork, short ribs, and chicken wings (four of each) when sautéing onions and garlic. If the sauce comes out a little on the acid side, use a pinch of baking soda to sweeten. Don't forget the meatballs.

Ingredients:

Salsa del Pomodori (Tomato Sauce)	15 oz.
Colla del Pomodori (Tomato Paste)	6 oz.
Aglio (Garlic)	3 Cloves
Cipolla (Onion)	1 Small
Olio di Oliva (Olive Oil)	3 Tbs.
Basilico (Basil)	10 Leaves
Prezzimolo (Parsley)	5-6 Leaves
Zucchero (Sugar)	1 Tsp.
Formaggio del Romano (Romano Cheese)	¼ Cup
Sale (Salt)	To Taste
Pepe Nero (Black Pepper)	To Taste
Aqua (Water)	15 oz.
Aqua (Water)	6 oz.

In a stockpot sauté finely chopped onion, minced garlic until translucent in oil. Add tomato paste and water. Cook until heated through. Combine tomato sauce, finely chopped fresh basil, fresh parsley, water, coarse black pepper, kosher salt and sugar in stockpot. Bring to boil stirring occasionally then simmer for about two to three hours. Stir in Romano cheese when sauce is done.

Optional: Add and blend ½ cup of Montepulciano with tomato paste and water or use chicken stock in place of water.

The Meatballs

(I Polpette)

Ingredients:

Vitello (Veal) Ground	½ lb.
Porco (Pork) Ground	½ lb.
Briciole del Pane (Bread crumbs)	⅔ Cup
Formaggio del Romano (Romano Cheese)	⅓ Cup
Uova (Eggs)	1 Large
Aglio (Garlic)	2 Cloves
Prezzimolo (Parsley)	2 Tbs.
Cipolla (Onion)	1 Small
Basilico (Basil)	10 Leaves
Olive di Oliva (Olive Oil)	3 Tbs.
Pepe Nero (Black Pepper)	To Taste
Sale (Salt)	To Taste

Mince garlic, onion, fresh basil and fresh parsley. Combine all ingredients in a large bowl. Form into balls about the size a little larger than a golf ball. Add oil to a large iron skillet, put in the meatballs and bake in the oven for 15–20 minutes (turning every five minutes) at 350 degrees F. Let meatballs cool then drop in spaghetti sauce that has been simmering for one hour. Continue cooking in sauce for at least one to two more hours.

NOTE: If mixtures a little dry, moisten with some olive oil before baking. Do not make mushy.

MENÚ DI NATALE

Contents

Cercese Digestive

APPETIZER

(ANTIPASTO)

Greased Bread Peasant Style

(A fallonte)

Ingredients:

Pancetta (Italian Bacon)	1 lb
Patate (Potatoes)	5 medium
Cipolla (Onion)	1 Large
Peperone Marinate (Marinated Peppers)	1 pint
Olio di Oliva (Olive Oil)	3 Tbs
Sale (Salt)	To Taste
Caldi del Pepe (Hot Pepper Flakes)	To Taste
Pane (Bread)	1 Loaf

Cut Italian Bacon into thick slices and sauté in olive oil. Boil the potatoes sliced until tender and add to the bacon. Add the chopped onion, pickled peppers, salt and hot pepper flakes.

Cook over low heat until all ingredients are heated through. Using a slotted spoon, scoop out the mixture on to individual plates. Pull the bread apart into large pieces and dip into the remaining oil to flavor and serve.

Granma's Soup

(Zuppe da Mammelle)

Ingredients:

Polpaccio (Veal Shank)	1 lb.
Cipolla (Onion)	1 small
Carota (Carrot)	1 small
Sedano (Celery)	1 stem
Indivia (Endive)	To Taste
Aqua (Water)	2 Qts.
Sale (Salt)	To Taste
Pepe Nero (Black Pepper)	To Taste
Pane (Bread) Cubed	
Scamorza or Mozzarella Cheese (Cubed)	

In a stockpot add the chopped veal shank, finely chopped onion, finely chopped carrot, finely chopped celery, salt, pepper and water. Bring to a boil reduce heat and cook until all ingredients are tender and done. Reduce heat. Take the meat out. Add endive and simmer lightly to just heat thoroughly. Fry the cubed stale bread to make croutons. Arrange the croutons in individual bowls and add some cubed scamorza or mozzarella cheese. Pour the soup into the bowls and serve.

First Course

(Primo Piatto)

Cavatelli with Pork Sauce

(Cavatieglie ca Carne de Puorche)

Ingredients:

Cavatieglie (Cavatelli)	1 lb
Nervature del Porco (Pork Ribs)	½ lb
Salsiccia Italiana (Italian Sausage)	½ lb
Rullo del Porco (Pork Roll)	½ lb
Pancetta (Italian Bacon)	½ lb
Cipolla (Onion)	1 small
Olio di Oliva (Olive Oil)	3 Tbs
Aglio (Garlic)	2 cloves
Prezzimolo (Parsley)	½ cup
Moscato (White Wine)	½ cup
Sale (Salt)	To Taste
Pepe Nero (Black Pepper)	To Taste

Make the pork roll by flattening the meat (between plastic wrap) with a mallet. Mince the garlic and coarse chop the fresh parsley. Spread the garlic and parsley mixture on the pork, roll and tie together with cooking thread. In a saucepan sauté the pork chops, sausage, pork roll, chopped bacon and chopped onion until brown in the oil. Sprinkle the meat with wine occasionally. Add spaghetti sauce and simmer for two hours. Sauce recipe on page 68. Cook the Cavatelli according to the instructions on the box for al dente.

SECOND COURSE

(SECONDO PIATTO)

Holiday Wild Game

(Gioco Selvaggio di Festa)

Ingredients:

Coniglio (Rabbit), Cinghiale (Wild Boar)

Capriolo (Venison) or Fagiamo (Pheasant)

Briciole del Pane (Bread Crumbs)	1 Cup
Cipolla (Onion)	1 Small
Aglio (Garlic) Minced	2 Cloves
Salvia (Sage)	1 Tbs
Rosmarino (Rosemary)	1 Tbs
Prezzimolo (Parsley)	1 Tbs
Caldi del Pepe (Hot Pepper Flakes)	To Taste
Limone (Lemon) Grated Zest	2 Tsp
Montepulciano (Dry Red Wine)	½ Cup
Olio di Oliva (Olive Oil)	3 Tbs
Sale (Salt)	To Taste
Pepe Nero (Black Pepper)	To Taste
Salsa di Soia (Soy Sauce)	2 Tsp

Instruction on the following page.

For this recipe, you can use one of the meats or a combination of meats. Cut meat into one-inch cubes (1 lb) and pound to tenderize.

In a bowl, mix meat, chopped onion, minced garlic, sage, rosemary, parsley, hot pepper flakes, salt, pepper and the red wine. Squeeze the juice of lemon over the mixture and add the soy sauce. Marinated at room temperature for a couple of hours or over night in the refrigerator.

Heat the olive oil in a heavy metal pan. Coat the meat (lightly) with bread-crumbs that has the lemon zest mixed in and add to the frying pan.

Fry the meat evenly (about 3-4 minutes) or until a little pink inside. Experience will have to guide you. Remove with slotted spoon onto a paper towel or loaf of bread that has been cut lengthwise (this is the old method to flavor the bread).

Remember, do not let the oil get to hot and if there are bare spots on the meat just sprinkle more breadcrumbs on the hot meat. Garnish with fresh rosemary, fresh sage and lemon slices.

Optional: This recipe can be used on any type of meat. Even on meatballs.

Stuffed Peppers

(Peperoni Farciti)

Ingredients:

Peperoni (Peppers)	6 medium
Vitello (Veal) Ground	½ lb
Porco (Pork) Ground	½ lb
Briciole del Pane (Bread Crumbs)	½ cup
Formaggio del Romano (Romano Cheese)	½ cup
Uova (Eggs)	1 large
Aglio (Garlic)	2 Cloves
Uva Passa (Raisins)	1 Small Box
Olio di Oliva (Olive Oil)	3 Tbs.
Sale (Salt)	To Taste
Pepe Nero (Black Pepper)	To Taste

Clean and core the peppers. Do not cut tops off. In a large bowl mix the breadcrumbs, cheese, eggs, minced garlic, salt, pepper and raisins. If a little dry, moisten with olive oil but do not make mushy. Fill the peppers through the core hole. Place in baking dish cover with the olive oil and bake at 350 degrees F for 30–35 minutes. Rotate the peppers ¼ turn while baking until all side are cooked.

Stuffed Artichokes

(Carciofi Farcito)

Ingredients:

Carciofi (Artichokes)	8 Small
Formaggio del Romano (Romano Cheese)	1 Cup
Briciole del Pane (Bread Crumbs)	1 Cup
Aglio (Garlic)	4 Cloves
Prezzimolo (Parsley)	2 Tbs.
Basilico (Basil) Chopped	10 Leaves
Olio di Oliva (Olive Oil)	8 Tablespoons
Sale (Salt)	To Taste

Clean the artichokes. Cut the top off and trim the leaves (cut off the tips), cut off the stems and remove the skin off the stems. Pound the artichokes on a flat surface holding the bottom in the palm of your hand to open the leaves. If the leaves are still pressed together, separate individually. Mince the garlic; combine with parsley, fresh basil, the Romano cheese and breadcrumbs. Fill the open leaves with the mixture. Place in pot with some water in it. Drizzle the olive oil over the artichokes and cover with a lid. Bake at 350 degrees F for one hour.

To eat these, you pull off each leave (one at a time) and holding the outer tip, you place the leave between your front teeth and while applying pressure you scrape the mixture off the leave. Once you get to the center be sure not to eat the 'choke' (spiny part) and finish this delicacy by enjoying the heart.

Optional: Add 1–2 beaten eggs to the mixture.

SALADS

(INSALATE)

Tossed Salad Family Style

(Insalata Stile Mista della Famiglia)

RECIPE ON PAGE 56.

Marinated Peppers and Olive Salad

(Insalata di Peperoni ed Oliva Marinati)

Peperone Marinate (Marinated Peppers)	2 Cups
Olive Curate Olio (Oil Cured Olives)	1 Cup
Cipolla (Onion)	1 Small
Sedano (Celery)	½ Cup
Aglio (Garlic)	1 Clove
Scorza Arancione Grattata (Grated Orange Rind)	2 Tbs.
Caldi del Pepe (Hot Pepper Flakes)	To Taste
Olio di Oliva (Olive Oil)	1 Oz.

Cube the peppers, dice the celery, cut the onion into small slices, and finely mince the garlic. Combine with the olives, grated orange rind and hot pepper flakes. Next pour on the olive oil, cover and refrigerate.

DESSERT
(DOLCI)

Christmas Wedding Cookie
(Biscotto Nunziale di Natale)

Ingredients:

Farina (Flour)	4 Cups
Uova (Eggs)	3 Eggs
Burro (Butter) Melted	¾ Cup
Latte (Milk)	½ Cup
Lievito (Baking Powder)	4 Tsp.
Sale (Salt)	½ Tsp.
Zucchero (Sugar)	¾ Cup
Vaniglia (Vanilla)	1 Tsp.

Mix the eggs, the butter and sugar together. Next add the milk and the vanilla. Sift the flour, salt and baking powder. Blend the dry ingredients with the wet ingredients. Roll into balls about the size of a golf ball. Place the balls on to a cookie sheet that has been greased and dusted with flour. Bake at 350 degrees F. until they are a light brown about 15 minutes. Let cool for about five minutes on a wire rack.. Cut cookie in half and fill with preserves of your choice and replace the top half. Coat with white or pastel icing. To make your own icing, whisk 2 ¼ tablespoons of milk, one tablespoon of egg whites and 1 ¼ cups of confectioners' sugar until smooth and creamy. Leave the icing white or divide and color with various food colorings. Keep in cool place for one hour before serving.

Optional: After icing sprinkle with coconut.

The Biscuits

(I Biscotto)

Ingredients:

Farina (Flour)	5 Cups
Lardo (Crisco)	1 Cup
Uova (Eggs) Beaten	2 Large
Zucchero (Sugar)	2 Cups
Aqua (Water)	1 Tbs.
Latte Acido (Sour Milk)	1 Cup
Bicarbonato di Sodio (Baking Soda)	1 ½ Tsp.
Vaniglia (Vanilla)	1 Tsp.
Anice (Anise)	1 Tsp.

Cream the Crisco, sugar, beaten egg and water. Next add the vanilla, anise, flour, baking soda and milk. Knead until all ingredients are incorporated. Make into small loafs about 4" x 12". Bake at 350 degrees F. for 20 minutes on a greased pan. Let cool. Slice into one-inch widths and serve.

Optional: Addition of fruits (cherries) or any other fruit of your choice can be added to the mixture prior to baking. Also, after slicing you can toast the slices for a short time and then serve.

Half Moon Pastry

(I Sciadune)

Ingredients:

Pastry:

Farina (Flour)	8 Cups
Lardo (Crisco)	1 ½ Cups
Uova (Eggs) Beaten	4 Large
Aqua (Water)	1 ½ Cups
Sale (Salt)	To Taste

Filling:

Uova (Eggs)	1 Dz.
Ricotta (Ricotta Cheese)	2 lbs.
Formaggio del Romano (Romano Cheese)	1 ½ lbs.
Salciccia Stagionata (Pepperoni)	2 Cups
Prosciutto (Ham)	2 Cups

The instructions for assembling pastry and filling are on next page.

To make the pastry—sift the flour onto a pastry board, work in the Crisco and lightly beaten eggs. Add a pinch of salt and the water. Knead to soft dough and let it set.

Next roll out the pastry to a thin layer on a lightly floured surface. Cut the layer of pastry into round shapes (12).

To make the filling—whisk the eggs in a large bowl, add the pepperoni and ham that have been diced. Stir in the Romano and ricotta cheeses. Mix to a firm texture.

Spoon the filling onto the pastry rounds and fold in half. Close the ends with a fork or a pastry wheel.

Next beat 1 egg and two egg yokes and brush the top surface of each sciadune. Prick the tops with a toothpick and bake at 350 degrees F until golden brown.

Optional: Use sugar (1 cup) instead of the meats and a dash of vanilla for the filling or reverse the amounts of the cheeses in the filling.

Our version for this type of pepperoni roll is uniquely Cercesi and brings out the soul of the Italian in everyone. Remember to fill your glass with more robust wine as the bite of the Romano cheese needs to be washed down or is this just an excuse to drink more wine.

PROVINCIAL WINES

(Vini Provinciali)

The heart of Italy is the historic hills where ample sunshine and temperatures are conducive to making flavorful and fine wines.

Grapes are grown mainly in the narrow coastal plains on the Adriatic side of the Molise and Abruzzo regions and the tortuous hills that are predominant in these regions of Italy. Two grapes, widely cultivated, make pleasant wines.

The tradition of wine making in Molise can be attributed to the Etruscans of the 7th and 8th centuries B.C. and the use of the Elm tree as a support for the grapevine is credited to them.

Montepulciano is deep rudy in color with an aromatic bouquet, robust full-bodied and dry. A very drinkable red wine that goes well with roasts and pasta. Even though Montepulciano is a remarkable wine on it's own, it has a natural affinity to be used more and more when blending with other fine red wines like Sangiovese.

The white Moscato is a perfumed light-bodied wine with a luscious, sweet "nose". This wine is very drinkable and goes well with light cheeses, fruits and desserts. Moscato can be used when making a syrup to pour over peaches or as a nice touch when cooking pork or veal. In the Molise province, producers of sparkling wines often use the Muscat grape to create wines in the style of Italian Spumante.

ITALIAN PROVERBS

(Proverbi Italiano)

A travola non s̀ invecchia—We do not age at the dinner table.

Amicizie e maccheroni, sono reglio caldi—Friendship and macaroni are best when warm.

Chi mangia bene, vive bene—Who eats well lives well.

Uva cattiva non fá buon vino—You can't make good wine from bad grapes.

Amici e vini sono meglio vecchie—Old friends and old wine are best.

Buona salute é la vera ricchezza—Good health is true wealth.

Al contadino non far sapere quanto é buono il formaggio con le pere.—Don't let the farmer know how good cheese is with pears.

Mangiare per vivere e non vivere per mangiare.—Eat to live and not live to eat.

Botte buona fa buon vino.—A good cask makes good wine.

Non si vive di solo pane.—One does not live by bread alone.

Troppi vini rovinano il cuoco.—Too many wines spoil the cook.

Io sono fame!
I'm hungry!

Grape Stalk

(Grappa)

Unlike brandy, which is distilled from wine, Grappa is distilled from the soul of the grape—the solids left behind when the juice of the grape starts on its journey to becoming wine.

After a large meal, Grappa is usually served in a tall shot glass and has an uncanny effect on the feeling of being full or bloated. The taste and aroma grows stronger as it matures and is an experience one will never forget. I call it 'firewater'.

To many Italians, grappa remains a folk remedy for toothache, bronchitis, and rheumatism. When it is done, the spent pomice is pressed into cakes, dried and used as fuel for the still. The ashes are returned to the vineyard as fertilizer and so the natural cycle is completed.

CONVERSION CHART

(Travole di Conversione)

Fluid

1 Fluid Ounce	30ml
4 Fluid Ounce	120ml
8 Fluid Ounce	240ml
12 Fluid Ounce	360ml
16 Fluid Ounce	480ml

Dry

¼ Teaspoon	1ml
½ Teaspoon	2ml
¾ Teaspoon	4ml
1 Teaspoon	5ml
1 Tablespoon	15ml
¼ Cup	60ml
½ Cup	120ml
1 Cup	240ml
2 Cups	480ml

Mass

¼ Teaspoon	1 ⅛ Grams
½ Teaspoon	2 ¼ Grams

1 Teaspoon	4 ½ Grams
½ Tablespoon	7 Grams
1 Tablespoon	14 Grams
¼ Cup	57 Grams
½ Cup	113 Grams
1 Cup	227 Grams
½ Quart	454 Grams
1 Quart	907 Grams

NOTE: 1 LITER EQUALS 34 FLUID OZ.

Oven Temperatures

(Temperatura del Forno)

250 Degrees F	120 Degrees C
275 Degrees F	140 Degrees C
300 Degrees F	150 Degrees C
325 Degrees F	160 Degrees C
350 Degrees F	180 Degrees C
375 Degrees F	190 Degrees C
400 Degrees F	200 Degrees C
425 Degrees F	210 Degrees C
450 Degrees F	230 Degrees C

GRAZIE

This book is dedicated to the immigrants from Cercemaggiore, Sepino, Riccia and Gildone. Four small hamlets located in the south central mountains of Italy.

These proud and noble people braved the unknowing by migrating to a new and different world with little money in their pockets. They worked hard long hours to build a new life and start new families. Never forgetting where they came from and the traditions that their ancestors started before them.

The Eve of Seven Fishes is a monument to their honor, dedication to family and the delectable authentic peasant recipes they brought to a little area of Greensburg, Pa. known as Hilltop.

I special thank you to my mother Julia (Spino) Germano, my father Michael Germano, my paternal grandparents Gaetano and Maria (Farinacci) Germano along with my maternal grandparents Vincenzo and Filomena (DeBone) Spino. Without their love, strength, customs and faith in God this cookbook of simple culinary classics would never have been composed.

Molte Grazie

Finally, thank you to the following surnames from Cercemaggiore, Sepino, Gildone and Riccia.

Panichella – Moffa – DeFloria – Felice – Pace – Zappone – Sabatine – DiOrio – Altieri – Reno – Rause – Testa – Salvatore – D'Amico – Rocco – D'Versa – Damato – DiPasquale – Delesandro – Ficco – Vaccaro – Cerelli – Cipullio – DeFabo – Cipriani – Pietrandrea – DiNiro – Miele – Sanzo.

EPILOGUE

Authentic Italian food comes to us by way of natural ingredients simmered together with love and the joy of feeding your family the finest cuisine in the world. Christmas Eve is a celebration to enjoy the gifts of family and food God gave all of us.

To savor that great Italian taste, visit DeLallo Fine Italian Foods when in Greensburg, Pennsylvania or Carlo's Italian-Delights Deli in Fairmont, WV.

Greensburg, Pa.
County of Westmoreland

Following the Revolutionary War, an inn was built along a wagon trail (today's East Pittsburgh Street) that stretched from Philadelphia west over the Appalachian Mountains to Fort Pitt, now Pittsburgh. A tiny settlement known as Newtown grew around the inn, today the intersection of Pittsburgh and Main Streets.

Indians burned Hannastown, the original Westmoreland County Seat north of Greensburg in 1782. Newtown became the new county seat in 1785. In 1786 the county built a log courthouse on land purchased from two residents, Christopher Truby and William Jack. Every Westmoreland County Courthouse since has stood on this site. The area surrounding the courthouse became the original borough of Greensburg, named for Revolutionary War General Nathaniel Greene and formally incorporated as a Borough in 1799.

In the 1970's, as shopping malls and new shopping centers appeared outside the City, Greensburg's downtown was adversely affected as large downtown stores closed. However, the City became a center for service industries, professional offices and banking. Today, small downtown shops and a growing number of restaurants are reviving downtown as a mercantile center. Larger shopping centers can be found at the edges of the City.

Reference: **http://www.city.greensburg.pa.us/**

INDEX

(Indice)

Recipe Index

(Indice di Ricetta)

Photography of Italy
by
Robert A. Germano

978-0-595-36510-4
0-595-36510-8

CPSIA information can be obtained at www.ICGtesting.com
Printed in the USA
BVOW041327091211

277959BV00002B/28/A